Emotional Intelligence Mastering Conflict Resolution and Negotiation

Seema

Emotional Intelligence Mastering Conflict Resolution and Negotiation

Copyright © 2023 by Seema

The first edition was published in 2023

ISBN:

Published by:
Sunshine
1663 Liberty Drive
Hyderabad, IN 47403
www.Sunshinepublishers.com

This book is self-published using on-demand printing and publishing, which allows it to be printed and distributed globally

TABLE OF INDEX

Chapter 1: Introduction to Emotional Intelligence and Conflict Resolution

Understanding Emotional Intelligence

Emotional Intelligence (EI) is a concept that has gained significant attention in recent years due to its profound impact on personal and professional success. In this subchapter, we delve into the depths of this fascinating subject, exploring what emotional intelligence is, why it matters, and how it can be developed and harnessed.

At its core, emotional intelligence refers to the ability to recognize, understand, and manage our own emotions, as well as the emotions of others. It involves being aware of our own emotional states and using this awareness to navigate social interactions effectively. Emotionally intelligent individuals possess a heightened sense of empathy, enabling them to understand and relate to others on a deeper level.

Why does emotional intelligence matter? Well, research has shown that EI plays a crucial role in various aspects of our lives. From personal relationships to leadership abilities, emotional intelligence influences how we handle conflicts, make decisions, and communicate effectively. It is a key factor in building and maintaining successful relationships, both at home and in the workplace.

Fortunately, emotional intelligence is not a fixed trait; it can be developed and enhanced over time with practice and self-reflection. In this subchapter, we will explore practical techniques and strategies for improving emotional intelligence, such as cultivating self-awareness, managing stress and emotions, and improving social skills.

Moreover, we will shed light on the benefits of emotional intelligence in conflict resolution and negotiation. By understanding and managing our emotions effectively, we can navigate difficult conversations and resolve conflicts with empathy and understanding. Emotional intelligence allows us to approach conflicts with a calm and rational mindset, fostering better communication and collaboration.

Throughout this subchapter, we will delve into real-life examples and case studies that highlight the importance of emotional intelligence in various contexts. By understanding the principles of emotional intelligence, we can harness its power to improve our personal and professional lives.

Whether you are a student, professional, or simply someone interested in personal growth, understanding emotional intelligence is essential. By developing this skill, you can enhance your relationships, become a more effective communicator, and navigate conflicts with confidence and grace.

Join us on this enlightening journey as we dive into the world of emotional intelligence, exploring its intricacies and discovering the transformative power it holds.

The Importance of Conflict Resolution and Negotiation Skills

In today's fast-paced and interconnected world, conflict is an inevitable part of our lives. Whether it be in our personal relationships, professional settings, or even within ourselves, conflicts can arise and disrupt our emotional well-being. This is where the importance of conflict resolution and negotiation skills comes into play.

Emotional intelligence, which encompasses our ability to recognize, understand, and manage our own emotions, as well as empathize with others, forms the foundation for effective conflict resolution and negotiation. By developing these skills, we can navigate conflicts more smoothly, maintain healthy relationships, and foster a positive and productive environment.

Conflict resolution refers to the process of addressing and resolving disagreements or disputes in a constructive manner. It involves recognizing the underlying issues, actively listening to others' perspectives, and finding mutually beneficial solutions. Without conflict resolution skills, conflicts can escalate, leading to heightened emotions, strained relationships, and even detrimental consequences.

Negotiation skills, on the other hand, are crucial in finding common ground and reaching agreements. Negotiation involves a give-and-take approach where both parties work towards a compromise that satisfies their interests. By honing negotiation skills, we can improve our ability to communicate effectively, build trust, and create win-win outcomes.

Emotional intelligence plays a vital role in conflict resolution and negotiation. It helps us understand our emotions, enabling us to remain calm and composed during conflicts. By managing our emotions, we can respond rather than react impulsively, which often leads to further conflict. Additionally, emotional intelligence allows us to empathize with others, understanding their perspectives and needs, and finding solutions that are acceptable to all parties involved.

For individuals seeking personal growth and self-improvement, developing conflict resolution and negotiation skills is essential. These skills empower us to express our needs, assert ourselves, and address conflicts in a healthy and respectful manner. They also foster stronger relationships, build trust, and enhance our emotional well-being.

In a professional context, emotional intelligence and conflict resolution skills are highly valued. Employers seek individuals who can navigate workplace conflicts effectively, collaborate with diverse teams, and contribute to a positive work environment. By mastering these skills, individuals can not only excel in their careers but also become effective leaders and agents of change.

In conclusion, emotional intelligence, conflict resolution, and negotiation skills are fundamental to our personal and professional lives. By investing in these skills, we can enhance our ability to manage conflicts, build stronger relationships, and create harmonious environments. The book "Emotional Intelligence: Mastering Conflict Resolution and Negotiation" serves as a valuable resource for anyone interested in developing these skills and harnessing the power of emotional intelligence.

Chapter 2: The Role of Emotional Intelligence in Conflict Resolution

Recognizing and Managing Emotions in Conflict Situations

Emotional intelligence plays a crucial role in conflict resolution and negotiation. In order to effectively navigate conflict situations, it is essential to recognize and manage emotions. This subchapter will provide valuable insights and practical techniques to help individuals enhance their emotional intelligence and effectively deal with conflicts.

Conflict situations often evoke strong emotions, such as anger, frustration, fear, or sadness. These emotions can cloud judgment and hinder rational decision-making. Recognizing and understanding these emotions is the first step towards effectively managing conflicts. By acknowledging our own emotions and those of others involved, we can gain valuable insights into the underlying issues and work towards a resolution.

One key aspect of recognizing emotions in conflict situations is self-awareness. This involves understanding our own emotional triggers, biases, and patterns of behavior. By being aware of our own emotions, we can better regulate them and prevent them from escalating conflicts further. Additionally, self-awareness allows us to empathize with others and understand their perspective, fostering a more collaborative approach to conflict resolution.

Managing emotions in conflict situations requires a set of skills known as emotional regulation. This involves effectively managing and expressing emotions in a manner that is constructive and respectful. Techniques such as deep breathing, taking a step back, and reframing negative thoughts can help individuals remain calm and composed during conflicts. By keeping emotions in check, individuals can approach conflicts with a more rational mindset, enabling them to find mutually beneficial solutions.

Furthermore, emotional intelligence involves recognizing and managing the emotions of others involved in the conflict. This requires active listening, empathy, and effective communication skills. By understanding the emotions and needs of others, individuals can tailor their approach and responses to foster a more positive and productive resolution.

Ultimately, recognizing and managing emotions in conflict situations is a fundamental aspect of emotional intelligence. By developing these skills, individuals can navigate conflicts with greater ease and achieve more successful outcomes. Whether in personal relationships, professional settings, or any other context, emotional intelligence is a crucial tool for mastering conflict resolution and negotiation. By honing these skills, individuals can build stronger relationships, foster collaboration, and create a more harmonious environment.

Empathy and Understanding in Conflict Resolution

In the realm of emotional intelligence, empathy and understanding play crucial roles in conflict resolution. When conflicts arise, it is natural for emotions to run high and for individuals to become fixed in their own perspectives. However, by cultivating empathy and seeking to understand the other party's point of view, we can foster a more harmonious and productive resolution.

Empathy is the ability to put ourselves in someone else's shoes and understand their feelings and experiences. It involves actively listening to the other person, acknowledging their emotions, and showing genuine care and concern. In conflict resolution, empathy allows us to create a safe space for open dialogue and to validate the other person's feelings, even if we do not agree with their perspective.

Understanding, on the other hand, goes beyond empathy and involves delving deeper into the underlying causes and motivations behind the conflict. By seeking to understand the other person's needs, fears, and desires, we can move beyond surface-level disagreements and work towards finding mutually beneficial solutions. Understanding requires active questioning, active listening, and a willingness to challenge our own assumptions and biases.

When empathy and understanding are incorporated into conflict resolution, several positive outcomes can be achieved. Firstly, it helps to de-escalate tensions and diffuse anger, as individuals feel heard and validated. This creates an environment of trust and openness, where both parties are more willing to explore potential solutions. Secondly, empathy and understanding allow for creative problem-solving, as different perspectives are considered and integrated. By embracing diverse viewpoints, new possibilities can emerge that were previously unseen.

To cultivate empathy and understanding in conflict resolution, several techniques can be employed. Active listening is essential, as it demonstrates genuine interest and allows for the accurate interpretation of the other person's emotions and needs. Reflective questioning can also be used to deepen understanding, by encouraging individuals to articulate their thoughts and feelings more clearly. Additionally, practicing self-awareness is vital, as it allows us to recognize and manage our own emotions, thereby preventing them from hindering the conflict resolution process.

In conclusion, empathy and understanding are key components of emotional intelligence that greatly contribute to conflict resolution. By fostering empathy, actively seeking to understand the other person, and embracing diverse perspectives, we can create a more harmonious and effective resolution process. Ultimately, the ability to empathize and understand others not only leads to successful conflict resolution but also enhances our overall emotional intelligence, enabling us to navigate future conflicts with greater ease and compassion.

Emotional Regulation Techniques for Conflict Resolution

In the realm of conflict resolution, emotional intelligence holds a crucial role in effectively managing and resolving conflicts. To master conflict resolution and negotiation, one must learn the art of emotional regulation. This subchapter aims to provide valuable techniques for emotional regulation, empowering individuals to navigate conflicts with grace and empathy.

1. Recognizing Emotional Triggers: The first step towards emotional regulation is recognizing our emotional triggers. By identifying specific thoughts, situations, or people that ignite intense emotions, we can proactively prepare ourselves for potential conflicts. Self-awareness is key to understanding how our emotions influence our behavior during conflicts.

2. Deep Breathing: When conflicts arise, our bodies often respond with heightened stress levels. Deep breathing exercises can help regulate our physiological responses by activating the parasympathetic nervous system, inducing a state of calmness. By taking slow, deep breaths, we can regain control over our emotions and think more clearly during conflicts.

3. Practicing Mindfulness: Mindfulness techniques, such as meditation or focusing on the present moment, can enhance emotional regulation skills. By observing our thoughts and emotions without judgment, we cultivate a non-reactive mindset, enabling us to respond to conflicts in a more thoughtful and compassionate manner.

4. Reframing Perspectives: Conflict resolution requires the ability to see multiple perspectives. By reframing our own thoughts and considering alternative viewpoints, we can foster empathy and understanding. This technique helps us detach from rigid positions, allowing for more open and productive discussions during conflicts.

5. Active Listening: Developing active listening skills is essential for emotional intelligence and conflict resolution. By truly listening to others, we validate their emotions and encourage open communication. Active listening involves giving our undivided attention, maintaining eye contact, and responding empathetically to the speaker's concerns.

6. Empathy and Validation: Empathy plays a pivotal role in emotional regulation during conflicts. By putting ourselves in the other person's shoes and acknowledging their emotions, we create a safe space for open dialogue. Validating someone's feelings does not mean agreeing with their perspective but rather demonstrating respect and understanding.

7. Taking Time-Outs: In heated conflicts, it is often beneficial to take a time-out to cool down and reflect. Stepping away allows us to regain emotional equilibrium, preventing impulsive reactions. During this break, it is important to self-reflect and consider the emotions and needs of all parties involved.

By implementing these emotional regulation techniques, individuals can enhance their conflict resolution skills and cultivate an atmosphere of understanding and cooperation. Emotional intelligence is the cornerstone of effective conflict resolution, enabling us to manage conflicts with empathy, assertiveness, and resilience. Mastering these techniques will empower individuals in both personal and professional settings, creating healthier and more harmonious relationships.

Chapter 3: Developing Self-Awareness for Effective Conflict Resolution

Self-Reflection and Understanding Personal Triggers

In the journey towards emotional intelligence, self-reflection plays a crucial role in understanding ourselves and managing our emotions effectively. By taking the time to reflect on our thoughts, feelings, and behaviors, we gain a deeper understanding of our own emotional triggers and can develop strategies to navigate conflicts and negotiations with finesse.

Self-reflection is not an easy task; it requires honesty, vulnerability, and a willingness to confront our own shortcomings. However, the rewards of this introspective practice are immeasurable. By examining our past experiences and current emotional responses, we can uncover patterns and triggers that influence our interactions with others.

One of the key aspects of self-reflection is identifying personal triggers. These triggers are specific situations, words, or actions that cause an immediate emotional response within us. They can stem from childhood experiences, unresolved traumas, or deeply ingrained beliefs. By recognizing our triggers, we can learn to respond rather than react, allowing us to maintain control over our emotions during conflict or negotiation.

Understanding personal triggers is the first step towards emotional intelligence. It provides us with the opportunity to engage in self-regulation, a crucial component of emotional intelligence. When we are aware of our triggers, we can implement strategies to manage them effectively. This might involve breathing exercises, taking a step back to gain perspective, or seeking support from a trusted friend or mentor.

Furthermore, self-reflection allows us to gain clarity about our own values and beliefs. By exploring our core values, we can align our actions and decisions with our authentic self. This alignment enhances our ability to communicate effectively, empathize with others, and find mutually beneficial solutions during conflicts and negotiations.

Self-reflection also fosters resilience and adaptability. When we take the time to understand our emotional triggers, we become better equipped to handle challenging situations. We develop an inner strength that allows us to bounce back from setbacks and navigate conflicts with grace and composure.

In conclusion, self-reflection is an essential tool in mastering conflict resolution and negotiation skills. It enables us to understand our personal triggers, regulate our emotions, and align our actions with our values. By engaging in self-reflection, we can develop emotional intelligence and enhance our ability to navigate conflicts and negotiations with confidence and success. So, take a moment to pause, reflect, and embark on the transformative journey of self-discovery.

Identifying and Managing Personal Biases

In the world of emotional intelligence, it is crucial to recognize and manage our personal biases. Biases are the preconceived notions and prejudices that we hold, often unconsciously, which can impact our decisions, actions, and interactions with others. These biases can cloud our judgment and hinder our ability to effectively resolve conflicts and negotiate with others. Therefore, it is essential to become aware of our biases and learn strategies to manage them.

The first step in identifying personal biases is self-reflection. Take the time to reflect on your beliefs, values, and experiences that may influence your perceptions and judgments. Consider how your upbringing and cultural background may have shaped your biases. By understanding and acknowledging these biases, you can begin to challenge and question them.

Another effective way to identify biases is through feedback from others. Seek input from trusted friends, colleagues, or mentors who can provide honest observations about your behavior and biases. Their perspectives can offer valuable insights that you may not have considered. Be open to receiving feedback without becoming defensive or dismissing their viewpoints. Remember, the goal is personal growth and improvement.

Once you have identified your biases, the next step is to manage them. One effective strategy is practicing empathy. Empathy allows us to see situations from the perspective of others, fostering understanding and reducing the influence of biases. Cultivate empathy by actively listening to others, considering their emotions and experiences, and putting yourself in their shoes.

Another powerful technique is cognitive reframing. This involves consciously challenging our biases by reframing situations in a more objective and balanced manner. For example, if you have a bias against a certain group of people, consciously challenge that bias by seeking out positive stories or experiences involving that group. This can help to counteract negative stereotypes and broaden your perspective.

Additionally, developing cultural competence is crucial in managing biases. Educate yourself about different cultures, beliefs, and worldviews. Engage in cross-cultural experiences, such as traveling or participating in diversity workshops, to gain a deeper understanding and appreciation for diversity.

Identifying and managing personal biases is an ongoing process. It requires self-awareness, introspection, and a commitment to personal growth. By acknowledging and challenging our biases, we can improve our emotional intelligence, enhance our conflict resolution skills, and become more effective negotiators. Ultimately, this leads to stronger relationships, better outcomes, and a more harmonious and inclusive world.

Self-Assessment Tools for Enhancing Emotional Intelligence

Understanding and developing emotional intelligence is crucial for anyone seeking personal growth and success in various aspects of life. Emotional intelligence refers to the ability to recognize, understand, and manage our own emotions, as well as those of others. By enhancing our emotional intelligence, we can improve our relationships, communication skills, and overall well-being. To help individuals on their journey towards emotional intelligence, various self-assessment tools have been developed.

One popular self-assessment tool is the Emotional Intelligence Appraisal. This tool allows individuals to assess their emotional intelligence across various domains, including self-awareness, self-regulation, empathy, and social skills. The appraisal provides a comprehensive report that highlights strengths and areas for improvement, enabling individuals to focus on specific aspects of emotional intelligence that require attention.

Another effective self-assessment tool is the Emotional Competence Inventory (ECI). Developed by renowned psychologist Daniel Goleman, the ECI measures emotional intelligence competencies such as self-awareness, empathy, adaptability, and influence. It provides a detailed analysis of an individual's emotional intelligence skills, allowing for targeted development and growth.

For those interested in a more introspective approach, journaling can serve as a powerful self-assessment tool. By dedicating time to reflect on our emotions, reactions, and interactions, we can gain valuable insights into our emotional intelligence. Journaling prompts can include questions such as "How did I handle a difficult situation today?" or "How did I show empathy towards others?" By regularly practicing self-reflection through journaling, we can track our progress and make necessary adjustments to enhance our emotional intelligence.

Additionally, the Emotional Quotient Inventory (EQ-i) is a widely used self-assessment tool that measures emotional intelligence competencies. It provides individuals with a comprehensive report on their emotional intelligence skills, outlining areas of strength and areas that require development. This tool can be particularly helpful for individuals who are looking for a detailed breakdown of their emotional intelligence abilities.

In conclusion, self-assessment tools are valuable resources for enhancing emotional intelligence. Whether through standardized assessments like the Emotional Intelligence Appraisal or the Emotional Competence Inventory, or through more introspective practices like journaling, individuals can gain valuable insights into their emotional intelligence skills and work towards improving them. By dedicating time and effort to self-assessment, anyone can develop and enhance their emotional intelligence, leading to more fulfilling relationships, effective communication, and overall personal growth.

Chapter 4: Building Empathy and Communication Skills

Active Listening Techniques for Conflict Resolution

In the realm of emotional intelligence, one crucial skill that can greatly contribute to conflict resolution and successful negotiation is active listening. Listening actively involves not only hearing the words being spoken but also understanding the underlying emotions, motives, and needs of the speaker. By employing active listening techniques, individuals can create a safe and empathetic space for resolving conflicts and promoting understanding.

One of the fundamental techniques of active listening is maintaining eye contact. When engaging in a conversation, it is essential to focus on the speaker and make eye contact. This demonstrates respect and genuine interest, fostering trust and openness. Additionally, maintaining eye contact helps to pick up non-verbal cues, such as facial expressions and body language, which can provide valuable insights into the speaker's emotions and intentions.

Another powerful technique is paraphrasing or summarizing the speaker's message. This involves restating the speaker's words in your own words to ensure comprehension and confirm understanding. Paraphrasing not only helps to clarify any potential misunderstandings but also shows the speaker that their message has been heard and respected. By summarizing the key points, it allows both parties to align their understanding and move towards a shared resolution.

Reflective listening is an active listening technique that involves repeating or reflecting the speaker's feelings and emotions. This technique allows the speaker to feel heard and understood, validating their emotions and promoting empathy. By reflecting emotions, individuals can create a deeper connection and build trust, which is essential for conflict resolution.

Furthermore, active listening involves asking open-ended questions to encourage the speaker to elaborate and provide more information. Open-ended questions invite dialogue and exploration, enabling a deeper understanding of the issue at hand. By asking questions such as "How do you feel about this situation?" or "What are your concerns?", individuals can uncover underlying emotions and needs, paving the way for effective conflict resolution.

In conclusion, active listening techniques are instrumental in conflict resolution and negotiation, and are a vital aspect of emotional intelligence. By maintaining eye contact, paraphrasing, reflecting emotions, and asking open-ended questions, individuals can create a safe and empathetic space for resolving conflicts and promoting understanding. These techniques foster trust, validation, and empathy, all of which are crucial elements in successful conflict resolution. By cultivating active listening skills, individuals can enhance their emotional intelligence and master the art of conflict resolution.

Non-Verbal Communication and Emotional Intelligence

Non-verbal communication plays a crucial role in our daily interactions, often speaking louder than words. It is an essential aspect of emotional intelligence, a skill that enables individuals to understand and manage their emotions effectively while also recognizing and empathizing with the emotions of others. In this subchapter, we will explore the intricate connection between non-verbal cues and emotional intelligence, and how mastering them can enhance our conflict resolution and negotiation abilities.

Non-verbal communication encompasses various forms, including facial expressions, body language, gestures, tone of voice, and even silence. These cues can convey emotions, intentions, and attitudes more accurately than verbal communication alone. For instance, a clenched fist or a furrowed brow can indicate anger or frustration, while a warm smile or open posture can signify friendliness and approachability. By learning to interpret these non-verbal signals, we can gain valuable insights into the emotional state of others and adjust our responses accordingly.

Emotional intelligence is about being aware of our own emotions and those of others, and utilizing that awareness to navigate social interactions effectively. The ability to accurately perceive and understand non-verbal cues is a key component of emotional intelligence. By being attuned to these signals, we can identify underlying emotions and respond with empathy and sensitivity. This heightened awareness allows us to build stronger connections, diffuse conflicts, and foster positive relationships.

Furthermore, non-verbal communication is instrumental in conflict resolution and negotiation. During conflicts, emotions often run high, and communication can become strained. In such situations, paying attention to non-verbal cues can provide valuable information about the emotions and needs of all parties involved. By tuning in to these signals, we can adapt our approach, showing empathy and understanding, which can help de-escalate tensions and promote a more collaborative environment.

In negotiations, non-verbal cues can also be powerful tools. Understanding the body language and tone of voice of the other party can provide insights into their level of interest, confidence, or even deception. By being aware of these cues, we can adjust our negotiation strategies accordingly, ensuring that our messages are received and understood effectively.

Another important aspect of empathy is perspective-taking. This involves stepping outside of your own viewpoint and attempting to understand the other party's perspective. By considering their values, beliefs, and experiences, you can gain valuable insights into their motivations and decision-making process. This understanding enables you to tailor your negotiation strategy and find creative solutions that meet both parties' interests.

In negotiation, perspective-taking is particularly crucial when conflicts arise. Instead of becoming defensive or aggressive, seek to understand the underlying reasons for the disagreement. By adopting a curious and open-minded attitude, you can uncover shared interests and common ground, ultimately leading to more fruitful negotiations.

Developing empathy and perspective-taking skills takes practice and self-awareness. It requires the ability to regulate your own emotions and set aside personal biases or preconceptions. By cultivating a genuine interest in others and a willingness to explore different viewpoints, you can enhance your emotional intelligence and become a more effective negotiator.

In summary, empathy and perspective-taking are essential components of emotional intelligence in negotiation. They enable you to connect with others on a deeper level, understand their needs, and find mutually beneficial solutions. By incorporating these skills into your negotiation approach, you can navigate conflicts more successfully and foster positive and long-lasting relationships.

Chapter 5: Emotional Intelligence Strategies for Negotiation

Emotional Preparation for Successful Negotiations

Negotiations are an integral part of our personal and professional lives. Whether we are discussing a salary increase, resolving a conflict, or finalizing a business deal, the ability to negotiate effectively is crucial. While many focus on the technical aspects of negotiation, such as strategy and tactics, it is equally important to recognize the role of emotional intelligence in achieving successful outcomes. Emotional preparation plays a significant role in our ability to navigate through negotiations with confidence, empathy, and resilience.

Emotional intelligence refers to the capacity to recognize and manage emotions, both in ourselves and others. It is a skill that can be developed and honed over time, and is a key factor in achieving positive outcomes in negotiations. Emotional preparation involves understanding our emotions, managing them effectively, and leveraging them to build rapport and influence others.

One essential aspect of emotional preparation is self-awareness. Before entering any negotiation, we must take the time to reflect on our own emotions and the potential triggers that may arise during the process. By understanding our emotional triggers, we can anticipate how they may impact our decision-making and ability to communicate effectively. Being aware of our emotions allows us to regulate them and make more rational and objective decisions.

Empathy is another critical component of emotional intelligence in negotiations. By putting ourselves in the shoes of the other party, we can better understand their needs, desires, and concerns. This understanding enables us to tailor our approach and proposals to effectively address their interests, ultimately fostering collaboration and win-win solutions. Demonstrating empathy also helps to build trust and rapport, making the negotiation process more productive and successful.

Resilience is a key characteristic of emotionally intelligent negotiators. Negotiations can be challenging and may involve setbacks and disappointments. Emotionally prepared negotiators are able to bounce back from setbacks and maintain focus on the ultimate goal. They are adaptable and can adjust their strategies as needed, without becoming overwhelmed by negative emotions. Resilience allows negotiators to persevere through difficult moments and ultimately achieve successful outcomes.

In conclusion, emotional preparation is a crucial aspect of successful negotiations. By developing emotional intelligence, we can enhance our self-awareness, empathy, and resilience, all of which contribute to more effective negotiation processes. Regardless of the context or niche, understanding and managing emotions is a vital skill that can lead to positive outcomes and strengthened relationships. By investing in emotional preparation, we can become more skilled negotiators and achieve greater success in our personal and professional lives.

Managing Emotions during Negotiation

In the fast-paced and competitive world of negotiations, emotions can often run high. Whether it is a business deal, a conflict resolution, or a personal discussion, the ability to manage emotions during negotiation is crucial for success. This subchapter aims to provide you with valuable insights on how to harness your emotional intelligence to navigate through negotiations effectively.

Emotional intelligence, often referred to as EQ, is the ability to recognize, understand, and manage one's own emotions, as well as the emotions of others. It plays a significant role in negotiation, as it allows you to remain calm, composed, and focused, even in the face of challenging situations. By mastering emotional intelligence, you can transform conflicts into opportunities and create win-win outcomes.

One of the key aspects of managing emotions during negotiation is self-awareness. Understanding your own emotions, triggers, and biases is essential in maintaining control over your reactions. By being aware of your emotional state, you can better manage your responses and avoid making impulsive decisions that may harm your negotiation position.

Furthermore, empathy is another crucial element of emotional intelligence when negotiating. By actively listening and understanding the perspectives, needs, and concerns of the other party, you can build rapport and trust. Empathy allows you to create a collaborative atmosphere, fostering open communication and increasing the chances of finding mutually beneficial solutions.

During negotiations, it is common for tensions to rise, and conflicts may emerge. It is important to remain composed and handle these situations with emotional intelligence. Instead of reacting impulsively, take a step back, and analyze the situation objectively. By reframing the conflict as an opportunity for growth and understanding, you can encourage a more constructive dialogue that leads to better outcomes.

Another valuable skill in managing emotions during negotiation is assertiveness. It is crucial to express your needs, concerns, and boundaries effectively while still respecting the other party's perspective. By maintaining a firm but respectful stance, you can assert your position without escalating tensions or damaging relationships.

In conclusion, mastering emotional intelligence is essential in managing emotions during negotiation. By cultivating self-awareness, empathy, assertiveness, and remaining composed under pressure, you can navigate through negotiations successfully. The ability to manage emotions not only enhances your negotiation skills but also enables you to build stronger relationships, resolve conflicts, and achieve mutually beneficial outcomes. By incorporating these strategies into your negotiation toolkit, you can become a master of emotional intelligence and excel in any negotiation setting.

Creating Win-Win Solutions through Emotional Intelligence

In today's fast-paced and interconnected world, the ability to navigate conflicts and negotiate effectively has become a crucial skill. Emotional intelligence, the capacity to recognize and manage our own emotions and understand the emotions of others, plays a vital role in mastering conflict resolution and negotiation. By harnessing emotional intelligence, individuals can create win-win solutions that not only address their own needs but also consider the needs and emotions of others involved.

Emotional intelligence is the key to fostering healthy and constructive relationships, both personally and professionally. It enables us to communicate effectively, empathize with others, and find common ground in the face of conflicts or negotiations. When emotions run high, rational decision-making often takes a backseat. By developing emotional intelligence, we can better regulate our emotions and make sound decisions that benefit all parties involved.

One of the fundamental aspects of emotional intelligence in conflict resolution and negotiation is empathy. By genuinely understanding and acknowledging the emotions of others, we can build trust, foster positive relationships, and find mutually beneficial solutions. Empathy allows us to step into someone else's shoes, see the situation from their perspective, and respond in a way that validates their emotions and needs.

Another crucial component of emotional intelligence is self-awareness. By being aware of our own emotions, triggers, and biases, we can better manage our reactions during conflicts or negotiations. Self-awareness helps us stay calm, composed, and focused, even in challenging situations. It allows us to approach conflicts with a clear mind, consider alternative viewpoints, and explore creative solutions that meet everyone's interests.

Moreover, emotional intelligence helps individuals cultivate effective communication skills. By being aware of our own emotions and actively listening to others, we can avoid misunderstandings, diffuse tensions, and find common ground. Effective communication involves not only expressing our needs and desires but also actively seeking to understand the needs and desires of others. By doing so, we can create win-win solutions that satisfy everyone's underlying interests and foster long-term cooperation.

In conclusion, emotional intelligence is a powerful tool for creating win-win solutions in conflict resolution and negotiation. By developing empathy, self-awareness, and effective communication skills, individuals can navigate conflicts with grace, build positive relationships, and reach mutually beneficial outcomes. Whether in personal relationships or professional settings, emotional intelligence is a skill that can enhance our lives, contribute to our success, and create harmonious and productive environments.

Chapter 6: Emotional Intelligence in Team Conflict Resolution

Understanding Group Dynamics and Emotional Intelligence

In today's fast-paced and interconnected world, the ability to navigate and understand group dynamics is crucial for success in both personal and professional settings. This subchapter aims to shed light on the importance of emotional intelligence in effectively managing group dynamics.

Group dynamics refer to the interactions and relationships that occur within a group. Whether it is a team at work, a social gathering, or a family unit, understanding how individuals interact with one another is essential for fostering positive relationships and achieving common goals. Emotional intelligence, on the other hand, refers to the ability to recognize, understand, and manage our own emotions, as well as the emotions of others.

Emotional intelligence plays a pivotal role in group dynamics as it enables individuals to effectively communicate, collaborate, and resolve conflicts. By being aware of one's own emotions and understanding how they can impact others, individuals can navigate group dynamics with empathy, respect, and authenticity.

One of the key aspects of emotional intelligence in group dynamics is self-awareness. Understanding our own emotions, strengths, weaknesses, and triggers allows us to manage our behavior and responses effectively. This self-awareness not only helps us regulate our emotions but also enables us to empathize with others, fostering a positive and inclusive group atmosphere.

Furthermore, emotional intelligence helps individuals build and maintain strong relationships within a group. By recognizing and understanding the emotions of others, individuals can adapt their communication and leadership styles to effectively connect with others. This empathy and understanding create trust and rapport, leading to a more cohesive and productive group dynamic.

Additionally, emotional intelligence equips individuals with the skills to navigate conflicts and disagreements within a group. Conflict is inevitable in any group setting, but emotional intelligence allows individuals to approach conflicts with empathy and open-mindedness. By understanding the emotions and perspectives of others, individuals can find common ground and negotiate win-win solutions, fostering a harmonious group dynamic.

In conclusion, understanding group dynamics and emotional intelligence is essential for anyone looking to navigate relationships and achieve success in various aspects of life. By developing emotional intelligence, individuals can build strong relationships, effectively communicate, and navigate conflicts within groups. By fostering a positive group dynamic, individuals can create an environment where everyone feels valued, heard, and motivated to work towards common goals.

Conflict Management Strategies within Teams

Conflict management is an essential skill within teams that can greatly impact the success and effectiveness of a group. In this subchapter, we will explore various conflict management strategies that can be employed to foster a positive and productive team environment.

Emotional intelligence plays a crucial role in conflict resolution within teams. It is the ability to recognize and understand emotions, both in oneself and others, and to effectively manage these emotions in a constructive manner. By harnessing emotional intelligence, team members can navigate conflicts with empathy, open-mindedness, and a focus on finding mutually beneficial solutions.

One effective strategy in conflict management is active listening. When team members feel heard and understood, they are more likely to engage in productive dialogue rather than escalating conflict. Active listening involves giving full attention to the speaker, seeking clarification, and summarizing what has been said. This approach helps to build trust and understanding within the team, leading to more effective conflict resolution.

Another important strategy is the use of assertive communication. Team members should feel comfortable expressing their needs, concerns, and perspectives in a respectful and direct manner. By being assertive, individuals can avoid passive-aggressive behavior or aggressive confrontation, which only further exacerbates conflicts. Assertive communication allows for open and honest dialogue, facilitating the identification and resolution of underlying issues.

Collaboration is also a key conflict management strategy within teams. Rather than approaching conflicts as win-lose situations, team members should aim for win-win outcomes. This involves actively seeking common ground, brainstorming alternative solutions, and working together to find a resolution that benefits all parties. By fostering a collaborative mindset, conflicts can be transformed into opportunities for growth and innovation within the team.

Lastly, it is important for team members to practice self-awareness and emotional self-regulation. Understanding one's own emotions and triggers allows individuals to respond to conflicts in a calm and controlled manner. By managing their own emotions, team members can prevent conflicts from escalating and find constructive ways to address and resolve issues.

In conclusion, conflict management strategies are crucial in maintaining a harmonious and productive team environment. By utilizing emotional intelligence, active listening, assertive communication, collaboration, and self-awareness, team members can effectively navigate conflicts and foster positive relationships within the team. Developing these strategies and skills will not only lead to better conflict resolution but also contribute to the overall success and emotional intelligence of the team.

Fostering Emotional Intelligence in Team Members

In today's fast-paced and interconnected world, emotional intelligence has become a critical skillset for individuals and organizations alike. It goes beyond the traditional measures of intelligence and technical expertise, instead focusing on an individual's ability to recognize, understand, and manage their own emotions, as well as effectively navigate and influence the emotions of others. In the realm of team dynamics, emotional intelligence plays a crucial role in fostering collaboration, enhancing communication, and ultimately driving success.

This subchapter delves into the importance of fostering emotional intelligence in team members and provides practical strategies to develop this skillset. Whether you are a team leader, a team member, or an individual looking to enhance your own emotional intelligence, this chapter will offer valuable insights and techniques.

First and foremost, fostering emotional intelligence starts with self-awareness. Team members must have a deep understanding of their own emotions, triggers, and patterns of behavior. By recognizing and managing their own emotions effectively, team members can create a positive and productive environment for collaboration. This chapter explores self-reflection exercises and techniques to help team members develop a heightened sense of self-awareness.

Additionally, emotional intelligence extends beyond self-awareness to include empathy and understanding towards others. Effective team collaboration relies on the ability to recognize and respond to the emotions and perspectives of fellow team members. This subchapter provides strategies and exercises to enhance empathy, active listening, and effective communication within the team.

Furthermore, emotional intelligence plays a significant role in conflict resolution and negotiation within teams. By understanding the emotions and needs of all parties involved, team members can find mutually beneficial solutions and prevent conflicts from escalating. This chapter explores techniques to manage conflict, negotiate effectively, and build consensus within a team setting.

Ultimately, fostering emotional intelligence in team members cultivates a more harmonious and productive work environment. It enhances team cohesion, boosts morale, and drives better decision-making. By investing in the development of emotional intelligence, individuals and organizations can unlock their full potential and achieve greater success.

Whether you are a team leader seeking to create a positive team culture or an individual looking to enhance your emotional intelligence, this subchapter offers invaluable insights and practical tools to foster emotional intelligence in team members.

Chapter 7: Emotional Intelligence in Difficult Conversations

Approaching Difficult Conversations with Emotional Intelligence

In today's fast-paced and interconnected world, mastering the art of emotional intelligence is crucial for successful conflict resolution and negotiation. Emotional intelligence refers to the ability to recognize, understand, and manage our own emotions, as well as effectively navigate the emotions of others. It is a skill that can be developed and honed over time, allowing us to approach difficult conversations with empathy, self-awareness, and a higher likelihood of reaching mutually beneficial outcomes.

Difficult conversations often arise in various aspects of our lives, whether it is with a colleague, family member, or friend. These conversations can be emotionally charged, filled with tension, and potentially lead to misunderstandings or further conflict if not handled with care. However, by applying emotional intelligence techniques, we can create an environment conducive to open dialogue and productive resolution.

One key aspect of emotional intelligence is self-awareness. Before entering into a difficult conversation, take a moment to reflect on your own emotions, triggers, and biases. By understanding your emotional state, you can better control your reactions and responses during the conversation. Additionally, acknowledging and managing your own emotions will allow you to approach the conversation with a calm and composed demeanor, setting the tone for a constructive discussion.

Empathy is another vital component of emotional intelligence. Put yourself in the other person's shoes and try to understand their perspective, concerns, and emotions. Actively listen to their words, body language, and tone, and respond with empathy and understanding. This approach creates a safe space for honest communication, fostering trust and reducing defensiveness.

During difficult conversations, it is important to stay focused on the issue at hand and avoid personal attacks or blame. Emotional intelligence allows us to separate the person from the problem, focusing on finding solutions rather than assigning fault. By maintaining a problem-solving mindset, we can explore different perspectives and brainstorm creative alternatives that can lead to win-win outcomes.

Finally, emotional intelligence helps us regulate our emotions and manage conflicts constructively. By staying calm and composed, we can avoid escalating the situation and instead guide the conversation towards a resolution. This requires active listening, managing our own emotions, and responding thoughtfully rather than reactively.

In conclusion, approaching difficult conversations with emotional intelligence is a powerful tool for conflict resolution and negotiation. By cultivating self-awareness, empathy, and a problem-solving mindset, we can create a safe and productive space for open dialogue. Emotional intelligence allows us to understand and manage our own emotions while empathetically responding to others, leading to mutually beneficial outcomes and improved relationships. By mastering emotional intelligence, we can navigate difficult conversations with grace and achieve successful conflict resolution in various areas of our lives.

Managing Strong Emotions during Difficult Conversations

In the realm of emotional intelligence, one of the most crucial aspects to master is managing strong emotions during difficult conversations. These conversations can be challenging, whether they are with a colleague, a friend, or a loved one. However, with the right strategies, it is possible to navigate these conversations effectively and maintain positive relationships.

Emotions play a significant role in shaping our responses during difficult conversations. When we are faced with conflict or disagreement, our emotions can intensify, making it difficult to think and communicate rationally. It is important to recognize and acknowledge our emotions without letting them control the conversation.

One effective strategy for managing strong emotions is to practice self-awareness. Take a moment to identify the emotions you are experiencing and understand their underlying causes. This will enable you to respond in a more composed manner, rather than reacting impulsively. Deep breathing exercises or a short meditation can help calm your mind and allow you to approach the conversation with more clarity.

Another important aspect of emotional intelligence is empathy. Putting yourself in the other person's shoes can help you understand their perspective and foster a more compassionate approach. By actively listening and validating their emotions, you can create a safe space for open dialogue and mutual understanding. Remember, difficult conversations are not about winning or losing, but about finding common ground and resolving conflicts.

During these conversations, it is also crucial to practice active communication. Clearly express your thoughts and feelings using "I" statements, rather than resorting to blame or criticism. Avoid interrupting the other person and focus on truly hearing their words. Non-verbal cues, such as maintaining eye contact and using open body language, can convey your engagement and willingness to find a resolution.

Lastly, don't be afraid to take breaks if the conversation becomes overwhelming. Stepping away for a few minutes can help you regain composure and perspective. It can also prevent the conversation from escalating into a heated argument.

Managing strong emotions during difficult conversations is a skill that takes time and practice to develop. By cultivating self-awareness, empathy, active communication, and knowing when to take breaks, you can navigate these conversations with emotional intelligence. Remember, the goal is to find resolution and maintain positive relationships, and mastering this aspect of emotional intelligence will greatly contribute to your overall success in conflict resolution and negotiation.

Resolving Conflicts and Rebuilding Relationships

In our journey through life, conflicts and disagreements are inevitable. They can arise in our personal relationships, within our families, at the workplace, or even in social settings. The way we handle these conflicts and navigate through them has a profound impact on our emotional intelligence and overall well-being. In this subchapter of "Emotional Intelligence: Mastering Conflict Resolution and Negotiation," we will delve into effective strategies for resolving conflicts and rebuilding relationships.

Conflict resolution requires a delicate balance of empathy, self-awareness, and effective communication. The first step towards resolving conflicts is to recognize and understand our own emotions and triggers. By developing our emotional intelligence, we can gain better control over our reactions and choose more constructive ways to express ourselves.

Active listening plays a crucial role in conflict resolution. It involves giving our full attention to the other person, understanding their perspective, and acknowledging their emotions. By doing so, we create a safe space for open conversation and demonstrate our willingness to find a resolution.

Another important aspect of conflict resolution is finding common ground. By identifying shared goals or interests, we can shift the focus from differences to areas of agreement, fostering collaboration and cooperation. This approach helps rebuild relationships and promotes mutual understanding.

Resolving conflicts also requires effective communication skills. It is important to express ourselves assertively, clearly stating our needs and concerns without attacking or belittling the other person. Using "I" statements helps to take responsibility for our emotions and avoids blame or defensiveness.

Forgiveness and empathy are essential for rebuilding relationships. Holding onto grudges or resentment only prolongs the conflict and hinders emotional growth. By practicing forgiveness, we let go of negative emotions and create space for healing and reconciliation.

Lastly, conflicts often provide opportunities for growth and self-reflection. By examining our own role in the conflict, we can learn from our mistakes and develop better strategies for future interactions. This self-awareness helps us build stronger emotional intelligence and fosters healthier relationships.

In conclusion, resolving conflicts and rebuilding relationships is a fundamental aspect of emotional intelligence. By understanding our emotions, actively listening, finding common ground, and practicing effective communication, we can navigate conflicts with grace and empathy. By fostering forgiveness and self-reflection, we not only resolve the conflict at hand but also grow personally and strengthen our relationships. Remember, conflict resolution is not about winning or losing, but rather about finding a middle ground where both parties can thrive.

Chapter 8: Enhancing Emotional Intelligence for Long-Term Conflict Resolution

Continual Development of Emotional Intelligence Skills

Emotional intelligence is a crucial skillset for anyone striving for personal growth and success in all aspects of life. It is the ability to recognize, understand, and effectively manage our own emotions and the emotions of others. In the book "Emotional Intelligence: Mastering Conflict Resolution and Negotiation," we delve into the importance of continual development of emotional intelligence skills and provide practical strategies to enhance this vital aspect of our lives.

The journey towards emotional intelligence is not a destination but a lifelong process. Just like any other skill, it requires consistent effort and practice to develop and refine. The subchapter "Continual Development of Emotional Intelligence Skills" aims to guide readers on this journey, helping them understand the importance of ongoing improvement and providing them with actionable steps to achieve it.

One of the key aspects of continuous emotional intelligence development is self-awareness. By becoming more aware of our own emotions, triggers, and patterns of behavior, we can take control of our reactions and make better decisions. This subchapter explores various techniques, such as self-reflection exercises and journaling, to foster self-awareness and gain insights into our emotional landscape.

Moreover, the subchapter emphasizes the significance of empathy in emotional intelligence. Empathy is the ability to understand and share the feelings of others, and it forms the foundation of meaningful relationships and effective communication. Readers will learn techniques to enhance their empathetic skills, such as active listening, perspective-taking, and nonverbal communication.

Another crucial aspect covered in this subchapter is emotional regulation. It is essential to manage our emotions effectively in various situations, especially during conflicts and negotiations. The subchapter provides practical strategies to develop emotional regulation skills, including deep breathing exercises, mindfulness techniques, and cognitive reframing.

Furthermore, this subchapter highlights the significance of continuous learning and growth in emotional intelligence. It encourages readers to seek feedback, engage in self-education, and embrace new experiences as opportunities for emotional development. By actively seeking out challenges and learning from both successes and failures, individuals can continuously improve their emotional intelligence skills.

In conclusion, the subchapter "Continual Development of Emotional Intelligence Skills" from the book "Emotional Intelligence: Mastering Conflict Resolution and Negotiation" serves as a guide for individuals of all backgrounds and professions who are interested in developing their emotional intelligence. Through self-awareness, empathy, emotional regulation, and continuous learning, readers will gain valuable insights and practical techniques to enhance their emotional intelligence skills and lead a more fulfilling and successful life.

Applying Emotional Intelligence in Different Conflict Situations

Emotional Intelligence: Mastering Conflict Resolution and Negotiation

Conflicts are an inevitable part of human interaction, and learning how to navigate through them with emotional intelligence can lead to more effective resolution and improved relationships. In this subchapter, we will explore how emotional intelligence can be applied in various conflict situations, empowering individuals to handle disagreements and disputes in a healthier and more productive manner.

Emotional intelligence, often referred to as EQ, involves the ability to recognize, understand, and manage our own emotions, as well as those of others. By harnessing these skills, individuals can develop strategies to address conflicts in a way that promotes understanding, empathy, and compromise.

One common conflict situation is within personal relationships. Whether it's a disagreement with a partner, family member, or friend, emotional intelligence can play a crucial role in resolving conflicts. By actively listening, acknowledging emotions, and demonstrating empathy, individuals can create a safe space for open and honest communication. This approach allows parties to express their thoughts and feelings, leading to a deeper understanding of each other's perspectives and finding common ground for resolution.

In the workplace, conflicts often arise due to differences in opinions, work styles, or misunderstandings. Emotional intelligence can help professionals navigate these situations more effectively. By managing their own emotions and remaining calm, individuals can avoid escalating conflicts and approach them with a level head. Additionally, understanding the emotions and motivations of colleagues enables individuals to find collaborative solutions, fostering a more positive and harmonious work environment.

Another area where emotional intelligence is crucial is in negotiations. Conflicts can arise during negotiations when parties have differing interests and objectives. By applying emotional intelligence, negotiators can build rapport, establish trust, and find mutually beneficial solutions. Understanding the emotions and needs of the other party allows for creative problem-solving and the development of win-win outcomes.

In conclusion, emotional intelligence is a vital skill set that can be applied in a variety of conflict situations, whether in personal relationships, the workplace, or negotiations. By developing our emotional intelligence, we can better manage our own emotions, understand others, and find common ground for resolution. This subchapter has explored the application of emotional intelligence in different conflict scenarios, providing valuable insights and strategies for readers to enhance their conflict resolution and negotiation skills.

Sustaining Positive Relationships through Emotional Intelligence

In a world where interactions and relationships form the foundation of our personal and professional lives, emotional intelligence plays a crucial role in cultivating and sustaining positive connections with others. The ability to understand and manage our own emotions, as well as perceive and empathize with the emotions of those around us, is at the heart of emotional intelligence.

Emotional intelligence allows us to navigate conflicts and negotiate effectively, leading to healthier and more fulfilling relationships. By harnessing this crucial skill set, we can foster open communication, resolve conflicts amicably, and build stronger connections with others.

One of the key elements of emotional intelligence is self-awareness. By developing a deep understanding of our own emotions, we can better respond to the emotions of others. This self-awareness enables us to recognize when our emotions may be clouding our judgment or impacting our interactions. By staying attuned to our emotional state, we can take a step back, reflect, and respond in a more thoughtful and constructive manner.

Empathy is another vital component of emotional intelligence. It involves putting ourselves in others' shoes and understanding their perspectives and emotions. By showing empathy, we can build trust and strengthen our relationships. People appreciate being heard and understood, and empathy allows us to provide the support and validation that others may need in challenging situations.

In order to sustain positive relationships, it is crucial to effectively manage conflicts and negotiate with others. Emotional intelligence allows us to approach conflicts with a calm and rational mindset, seeking mutually beneficial solutions. By reframing conflicts as opportunities for growth and understanding, we can find common ground and resolve disputes in a way that strengthens our relationships rather than damaging them.

Moreover, emotional intelligence enables us to communicate assertively yet respectfully. It empowers us to express our needs and boundaries while remaining considerate of others' feelings. This balance between assertiveness and empathy forms the foundation for healthy and effective communication, fostering positive relationships based on trust and understanding.

In conclusion, emotional intelligence is a vital skill set for sustaining positive relationships. By cultivating self-awareness, empathy, and effective conflict resolution skills, we can nurture stronger connections, both personally and professionally. By harnessing the power of emotional intelligence, we can master conflict resolution and negotiation, leading to more fulfilling and harmonious relationships in all areas of our lives.

Chapter 9: Case Studies: Applying Emotional Intelligence to Conflict Resolution and Negotiation

Case Study 1: Resolving Workplace Conflicts through Emotional Intelligence

Introduction:

In today's fast-paced and interconnected world, conflicts are inevitable, especially in the workplace. However, what sets successful professionals apart is their ability to navigate and resolve conflicts effectively. This subchapter presents a case study that demonstrates how emotional intelligence can play a pivotal role in resolving workplace conflicts.

Case   Study:

Meet Sarah, a highly skilled marketing manager who leads a team of diverse individuals. Despite her expertise, Sarah frequently encounters conflicts within her team. She notices that these conflicts not only hinder productivity but also dampen team morale. Determined to find a solution, Sarah decides to apply emotional intelligence principles to address the conflicts.

Firstly, Sarah recognizes the importance of self-awareness. She takes a step back and assesses her own emotions and reactions to the conflicts. By understanding her own triggers and biases, she becomes more open to listening to others' perspectives and avoids reacting impulsively. Sarah realizes that her own emotions can influence the team dynamics and decides to lead by example.

Next, Sarah focuses on building empathy among her team members. She encourages open and honest communication, creating a safe space for team members to express their concerns and emotions. Through active listening and understanding, Sarah helps her team members develop a deeper understanding of each other's viewpoints, fostering a sense of empathy and compassion.

Moreover, Sarah emphasizes the importance of emotional regulation. She encourages her team to manage their emotions constructively and avoid letting negative emotions escalate conflicts further. Sarah introduces techniques such as deep breathing exercises and stress management strategies to help her team members stay calm and composed during challenging situations.

Furthermore, Sarah promotes effective communication and conflict resolution skills. She conducts workshops and training sessions to enhance her team's interpersonal skills, including active listening, assertiveness, and compromise. By equipping her team with these skills, Sarah empowers them to resolve conflicts amicably, fostering a positive work environment.

Results   and   Conclusion:
Through implementing emotional intelligence principles, Sarah witnesses a transformation within her team. Conflicts are resolved more efficiently, and team members communicate and collaborate better than ever before. The overall work environment becomes more harmonious, leading to improved productivity and job satisfaction.

This case study exemplifies the power of emotional intelligence in resolving workplace conflicts. By developing self-awareness, empathy, emotional regulation, and effective communication skills, professionals can successfully navigate conflicts and foster positive working relationships. By mastering emotional intelligence, anyone can enhance their conflict resolution and negotiation abilities, leading to personal and professional growth.

Case Study 2: Negotiating Successful Business Deals with Emotional Intelligence

Introduction:

In today's fast-paced and competitive business world, negotiation skills are essential for success. However, merely relying on traditional negotiation tactics may no longer be enough. Emotional intelligence, often referred to as EQ, is a crucial factor that can significantly impact negotiation outcomes. This case study explores the application of emotional intelligence in negotiating successful business deals.

Understanding Emotional Intelligence: Emotional intelligence refers to the ability to recognize, understand, and manage one's own emotions, as well as the emotions of others. It involves empathy, self-awareness, self-regulation, social skills, and motivation. By harnessing emotional intelligence, negotiators can create a positive and collaborative environment, leading to win-win outcomes.

The Importance of Emotional Intelligence in Negotiation: Negotiating successful business deals requires more than just strategic thinking and assertiveness. Emotional intelligence allows negotiators to build rapport, establish trust, and effectively manage conflicts during the negotiation process. It enables them to understand the needs and desires of all parties involved, ultimately leading to mutually beneficial agreements.

Case   Study   Example:
Let's consider a case study involving two companies negotiating a merger. Both companies have strong positions and are seeking maximum gains. However, tensions rise due to conflicting interests and differences in corporate cultures. Traditional negotiation approaches fail to bridge the gap between them.

Applying   Emotional   Intelligence:
A negotiator with high emotional intelligence steps in to facilitate the negotiation process. They actively listen to the concerns of both parties, demonstrating empathy and understanding. By acknowledging the emotions and underlying motivations behind each party's demands, they create a safe space for open communication.

The negotiator utilizes their emotional intelligence skills to manage conflicts effectively. They remain composed and regulate their emotions, even in the face of high-stress situations. By doing so, they model emotional intelligence, encouraging the other negotiators to follow suit.

The   Outcome:
Through the application of emotional intelligence, the negotiator helps both companies find common ground and align their goals. They emphasize the shared benefits of the merger, highlighting how it can enhance the strengths of both organizations. By fostering positive relationships and trust, they create a win-win situation for both parties, resulting in a successful business deal.

Conclusion:

This case study highlights the significance of emotional intelligence in negotiation. By incorporating emotional intelligence skills, negotiators can better understand the needs and emotions of all parties involved, resulting in more successful and mutually beneficial business deals. Developing emotional intelligence is a valuable investment for anyone seeking to enhance their negotiation skills and achieve positive outcomes in various professional settings.

Case Study 3: Applying Emotional Intelligence in Personal Relationships

In this subchapter, we will delve into the practical application of emotional intelligence in personal relationships. Emotional intelligence plays a vital role in building and maintaining healthy connections with our loved ones. Whether it's our partner, family members, or close friends, understanding and managing emotions effectively can significantly enhance the quality of our relationships.

Let's take the example of Sarah and John, a married couple facing communication challenges due to their differing emotional needs. Sarah, an introvert, tends to withdraw when feeling overwhelmed, while John, an extrovert, seeks validation and attention during such times. This mismatch in emotional expression often leads to misunderstandings and conflicts.

By applying emotional intelligence, Sarah and John can bridge this gap and foster a more harmonious relationship. Firstly, they need to develop self-awareness by recognizing their own emotional triggers and understanding how they respond to stress. Sarah can learn to communicate her need for space to John, while John can practice offering support without overwhelming her.

Next, both Sarah and John should focus on enhancing their empathy skills. Empathy allows individuals to understand and relate to the emotions and experiences of others. Sarah can work on empathizing with John's need for reassurance and actively listen to his concerns. Conversely, John can strive to understand Sarah's need for solitude and give her the space she requires without feeling rejected.

Building on their self-awareness and empathy, Sarah and John can then cultivate effective communication strategies. They can learn to express their emotions clearly and honestly, using "I" statements to avoid blame and criticism. By communicating their needs and concerns openly, they can find common ground and devise mutually beneficial solutions.

Moreover, it is crucial for Sarah and John to develop emotional regulation skills. This entails managing and controlling their emotions in a healthy and constructive manner. Sarah can practice self-soothing techniques to calm herself during times of stress, while John can work on expressing his emotions without becoming defensive or aggressive.

Through consistent practice of emotional intelligence in their personal relationship, Sarah and John will notice a positive shift. They will become more attuned to each other's emotional needs, leading to increased understanding, empathy, and overall satisfaction in their relationship.

This case study demonstrates how emotional intelligence can be applied in personal relationships to navigate conflicts, improve communication, and foster deeper connections. By investing in emotional intelligence skills, individuals can enhance their relationships and create a nurturing environment for emotional growth and fulfillment.

Chapter 10: Conclusion and Future Applications of Emotional Intelligence

Recap of Key Concepts in Emotional Intelligence and Conflict Resolution

In the fast-paced and interconnected world we live in, emotional intelligence and conflict resolution skills have become essential for individuals to navigate their personal and professional lives successfully. This subchapter aims to provide a concise recap of the key concepts in emotional intelligence and conflict resolution, helping readers understand and apply these principles in their daily interactions.

Emotional intelligence refers to the ability to recognize, understand, and manage our own emotions and those of others effectively. It encompasses skills such as self-awareness, self-regulation, empathy, and social skills. Developing emotional intelligence allows individuals to foster better relationships, build trust, and handle conflicts in a constructive manner.

Self-awareness is the foundation of emotional intelligence. It involves understanding our own emotions, strengths, weaknesses, and triggers. By being aware of our emotions, we can better manage them and prevent them from negatively impacting our interactions and decision-making processes.

Self-regulation is the ability to control and manage our emotions in challenging situations. It requires identifying and managing stress, practicing mindfulness, and developing healthy coping mechanisms. By mastering self-regulation, individuals can respond rather than react to conflicts, leading to more productive outcomes.

Empathy is the ability to understand and share the feelings of others. It involves active listening, observing non-verbal cues, and putting ourselves in someone else's shoes. Cultivating empathy allows us to connect with others on a deeper level, build rapport, and find collaborative solutions during conflicts.

Social skills are the culmination of emotional intelligence, enabling effective communication and relationship building. These skills include assertiveness, active listening, and conflict resolution techniques. By developing strong social skills, individuals can express their needs and concerns assertively, listen actively to others, and find mutually beneficial solutions in conflicts.

Conflict resolution is the process of addressing disagreements and finding solutions that satisfy all parties involved. It requires effective communication, negotiation skills, and the ability to manage emotions. By employing collaborative problem-solving techniques, individuals can turn conflicts into opportunities for growth and strengthen relationships.

In conclusion, emotional intelligence and conflict resolution skills are vital for individuals in any field or stage of life. By recapitulating these key concepts, this subchapter aims to empower readers to enhance their emotional intelligence, navigate conflicts effectively, and build healthier and more fulfilling relationships. By applying these principles, individuals can become better leaders, negotiators, and contributors to a harmonious society.

The Future of Emotional Intelligence in Conflict Resolution and Negotiation

In today's fast-paced and interconnected world, the ability to navigate conflicts and negotiate effectively has become an essential skill for success in both personal and professional realms. Emotional intelligence (EI) plays a crucial role in these processes, and its importance is only expected to grow in the future.

Emotional intelligence refers to the ability to recognize, understand, and manage our own emotions, as well as the emotions of others. It involves empathy, self-awareness, self-regulation, and effective communication. These skills are invaluable in conflict resolution and negotiation, as they allow individuals to navigate difficult conversations, build trust, and find mutually beneficial solutions.

As we look to the future, emotional intelligence will become even more critical in conflict resolution and negotiation for several reasons. First, with the rise of technology and globalization, we are increasingly interacting with people from diverse backgrounds and cultures. Understanding and managing emotions across cultural boundaries will be vital in resolving conflicts and reaching agreements.

Additionally, the future workforce is expected to become more automated, with a greater emphasis on interpersonal skills. As machines take over routine tasks, emotional intelligence will become a key differentiator for individuals in the job market. Employers will value those who can effectively manage conflicts and negotiate with empathy and diplomacy.

Furthermore, the future of conflict resolution and negotiation will likely involve more virtual interactions. As remote work and virtual meetings become more prevalent, individuals will need to develop emotional intelligence skills that can be effectively applied in digital spaces. This includes understanding and managing emotions in written communication, video conferences, and other virtual platforms.

To prepare for this future, individuals should invest in developing their emotional intelligence. This can be done through self-reflection, seeking feedback from others, and engaging in training programs or workshops focused on emotional intelligence. By honing these skills, individuals can become better equipped to navigate conflicts, negotiate effectively, and build strong relationships.

In conclusion, emotional intelligence will play a crucial role in the future of conflict resolution and negotiation. As our world becomes increasingly connected and automated, individuals with strong emotional intelligence skills will be better equipped to navigate diverse cultures, stand out in the job market, and excel in virtual interactions. Investing in the development of emotional intelligence is a wise choice for anyone looking to master conflict resolution and negotiation in the future.

Implementing Emotional Intelligence Strategies for Personal and Professional Growth

Emotional intelligence is a key factor in personal and professional success. It is the ability to recognize and manage our own emotions and those of others. By developing emotional intelligence, individuals can enhance their communication skills, build stronger relationships, and navigate conflicts more effectively. This subchapter aims to provide valuable insights and strategies to help readers implement emotional intelligence in their lives for personal and professional growth.

In this subchapter, we will explore various strategies for developing emotional intelligence. Firstly, we will delve into self-awareness, which is the foundation of emotional intelligence. By understanding our own emotions, strengths, and weaknesses, we can better manage our reactions in various situations. We will discuss techniques such as self-reflection, journaling, and mindfulness practices that can enhance self-awareness.

Next, we will focus on self-regulation, which involves managing our emotions and impulses. This skill is crucial in maintaining composure during stressful situations and making rational decisions. We will discuss strategies such as deep breathing exercises, visualization, and positive self-talk that can aid in self-regulation.

Furthermore, we will explore empathy, the ability to understand and share the feelings of others. Developing empathy allows individuals to build stronger relationships, resolve conflicts, and demonstrate compassion. We will provide practical exercises and tips to enhance empathy, such as active listening and perspective-taking.

The subchapter will also cover social skills, which are essential for effective communication and relationship-building. We will discuss strategies for improving communication, assertiveness, and conflict resolution techniques. By enhancing social skills, individuals can foster healthier and more collaborative professional and personal relationships.

Throughout the subchapter, we will provide real-life examples and case studies to illustrate the practical application of emotional intelligence strategies. Readers will gain a deeper understanding of emotional intelligence and how it can positively impact their lives.

Whether you are a professional seeking to advance your career, a student navigating relationships, or simply someone interested in personal growth, implementing emotional intelligence strategies can lead to remarkable improvements. By mastering emotional intelligence, individuals can effectively manage conflicts, negotiate more successfully, and foster healthier relationships. This subchapter will equip readers with the necessary tools and insights to implement emotional intelligence strategies for personal and professional growth.

9 788119 669455